LETTERS TO MY PRESIDENT

El Hadji Malick Ndiaye

LETTERS TO MY PRESIDENT

Translated from the French
by Annie Jamison & Kenny Bates

Peregrine Press

Originally published in French as *Lettres à un président africain.*

Published by Peregrine Press
4124 39th Avenue SW
Seattle, Washington 98116
peregrinepress.us

ISBN: 979-8-9948941-1-8

Printed in the United States of America

Cover Design and Illustration by Annie Jamison

This text is pure fiction.

Any resemblance to real people, living or dead,
is purely coincidental.

"It is not titles that honor men,
but men that honor titles."

— Machiavelli

PREFACE

The undertaking that El Hadji Malick Ndiaye embarks upon in this correspondence he seeks to establish with the leader of an undoubtedly fictional African nation, is both demanding in its construction and urgently necessary in an unstable continental environment dominated by violent operations rather than deliberation. These circumstances plunge into the depths of the absurd, rendering meaningless the repeated calls for "peace," "national harmony," and "dialogue" that echo through cities and villages. Much has been written on the genealogy of power; photography has documented it; painting, too, is starting to bring it to light and convey its lessons. By retracing the adventures of the construction of power and institutions in African states, this correspondence brings intimacy and immediacy to the body of works devoted to systems of domination, accumulation of wealth, and repression.

The five letters take on the tone of a narrative composed by candlelight, in the secret music of confession; they excavate without compromise the recesses of a geography whose primary function is to blind and disorient the citizen within labyrinths saturated with deceptive fabulations. The letters draw from precolonial, colonial, and postcolonial histories. They move to the rhythms of traditional, religious, and modern melodies—serenades that rise, at times with mischievous seduction, always with obscene violence over diseased and famished bodies, perpetually poised for rebellion, withdrawal, and delinquency—often simply for indignity and surrender. Ndiaye does not merely sketch the portrait of an African head of state, rendered with a sure line and without acrimony. He also charts the trajectories unfolding within a deeper disorder: bloated and discordant institutions; economic and social policies that are opportunistic, discontinuous, and bound by a single constant: the explicit interweaving of public and private spheres. We are left with a patrimonial logic that reduces public space to the president's familial concession.

In a confiding tone that is both intimate and candid, Ndiaye chronicles a slow descent into the hells of authoritarianism, violence, deceit, and arrogance, which justify the narrator's defiance. This chronicle reveals the repeated operations, carried out with great fanfare, that darken the horizons of what has become an African political nightmare. These operations include the use of weapons, manipulated electoral processes, and doctored constitutions, in order to preserve power and subjugate citizens. Ndiaye's writing seamlessly weaves stark statistical precision with poetic expression of ever-vivid hopes, and a range of voices emerge as a result: exuberant laughter, unabashed and indecent commands, mocking sneers. The chronicle invites the reader to join in the macabre choreography of the men who merrily trample the tireless work of citizens who have managed to keep alive the dying light of democracy.

Most importantly, these letters powerfully illustrate the fierce resistance of the spark of democracy, kept alive by the youth who fight to escape the nightmare of tropical dictatorships led by ageless patriarchs. Dictators born in the interwar period when the colonial administration was gaining power and the dawn (now dusk) of postcolonialism was breaking. Dictators convinced that they are messiahs, masters and owners of nature and the communities they govern, messengers of a prophetic educational mission. Dictators who graced us with gleaming infrastructure, highways, bridges, tunnels, stadiums and arenas galore, a high-speed train.

Ndiaye does not simply offer a scathing assessment of the squandering of material and immaterial resources. In response to the fables whispered into the ear of the omnipresent, omniscient, and omnipotent president, the author offers an "age-old truth [...] that has been expressed in the markets, in the cafés, in the stadiums, in the mosques, in the fields, and in the factories for a long time now." To the political economy of "second-hand modernity"* displayed by infrastructure, airports, highways, and other modernization policies of the holy cities, he opposes an uncompromising ethnography of "the afflictions that are ravaging our country." Through successive strokes that establish parallels, interconnections, and juxtapositions, Ndiaye does not simply describe an ethnography that pits the elites against their subjects. He instead deciphers, with irony and profound sensitivity, the intricate dynamics between the different communities inhabiting the continent. The author wonders if these political leaders share the same cultures, political values, morals, and civic principles of their fellow citizens. He thus presents a vibrant portrayal of the conflicts, illusions, and glimmers of hope in societies engaged in a feverish quest for a brighter future.

These letters also explore the resurgence of an African youth that radically challenges the power structures through which more than four generations of African leaders—claiming a double heritage, real or invented, precolonial and colonial—have imagined a postcolonial president that is at once festive, nepotistic and repressive. Ndiaye reveals the emergence of a vision that breaks with the authoritarian

* Alf Schwarz, Le tiers monde et sa modernité de seconde main. Fundação José Augusto, 1982. [The Third World and Its Second-Hand Modernity.]

excesses produced by the accumulation of various norms of gender, generation, and colonial governance; the directives of the single-party system and its transformations into electoral democracies without political alternation or alternatives, and the pervasive violence used by the ruling elites to ensure the stability of the regime. The whispers and apathy that marked the political sequences of the first decades after independence have given way to the civic engagement of these youth. They have launched an assault on institutions burdened by the political, economic, and ideological alliances of diverse local and international forces. They have mobilized to bring about the collapse of the "system," a colonial legacy that never ceases to reinvent itself.

Ndiaye's letters compose a biography of the system that has kept Africa on the margins of the path leading to progress, democracy, and social justice—in short, an open society that is capable of providing for its men, women, and children. They reveal the marks left on the landscape, the barren forests and ravaged lands, the bodies of women and men, their hearts and minds, the blood, cries, and pain of the victims. All of these furrows welcome the seeds of a brighter tomorrow.

Mamadou Diouf
Columbia University, New York
March 2024

LETTER ONE

Mr. President,

I am writing to you with news from our country. I will send my letter to the local post office or publish it in the press, as I never know where to reach you. The presidential palace, which you so splendidly renovated upon your arrival, is empty eleven months out of the year, and your marble vacation house in the village where you were born echoes with an unsettling silence most of the time. It would be just as risky to address you at your Swiss chalet, your villa in Saint-Tropez, your chateau in the Périgord, your Parisian townhouse, or at some apartment in Monaco or New York. You are known to frequent these places but you're only there sporadically. As I'm writing to you, you might very well be somewhere in the sky or in an air-conditioned tent in the middle of the Arabian desert, if not at the luxurious dacha belonging to your new friend from the East, in the arms of those milky beauties you adore. Malicious tongues say the only way to escape you is to hide in your closet. Even the Devil, your acolyte, has decided to stop looking for you in this world and to wait patiently for you in his kingdom (where, I'm sure, you're not about to join him). Wherever you may be, I hope that this missive finds you in peace and joy, like the rest of your peers in Africa. It doesn't seem like a bad deal to be President in our part of the world, even if the adventure doesn't always have a happy ending. Because, even if presidents in other countries don't complain either, the job in Africa is extremely simple. You rule.

I would have preferred to address you in a direct, natural, and friendly manner, but given that we live in different worlds, this letter is the only reasonable space where my words can force their way through the unfathomable pathways of your mind. I have no doubt, Mr. President, that you will hear about my correspondence even though you are not a fervent admirer of the written word. No one has ever claimed to see you read a book. Why bother? You know everything. You can do everything. You have already said all there is to say. Surely, if you chose to read everything written about you each year, 365 days would not be enough and then it would cut into your vacation time. I remain hopeful that someone will read these few lines for you or that you yourself will be inspired to scan the neat and succinct summary given to you by your abundance of

Western advisors. *They* read. And maybe that's why they are in a position to advise you. However, I must admit to you from the outset that what I write here is a far cry from the simpering trumpets you are used to. You may even be shocked by my insolent tone and see me as a malicious, naïve, and irresponsible nobody who has allowed himself to be manipulated by your many enemies around the world. But Mr. President, these words come from the depths of my being. I am naïve enough to believe they are sincere and that they are not intended to attack you but rather to make you hear the voices of the weakest. Failing that, I would still like to tell you that what I express here is very close to what is whispered at night in the darkened homes of our young nation. It is an age-old truth that I hope will still bear fruit. It is the same truth that has been expressed in the markets, in the cafés, in the stadiums, in the mosques, in the fields, and in the factories for a long time now. Your advisors do not tell you this truth. They tell you the other thing you want to hear, that of your immense greatness and of the painfully happy people who support you. Flattering words, cloying words, lying words. I am addressing you with the words of the streets, not their words. And I realize that for someone who enjoys flattery, these are not pleasant words to hear.

Truthfully, I hesitated in writing to you and not only because you do not tolerate criticism. The first reason—which seemed obvious to me—is your omniscience, which means that you do not listen to anyone, no matter if they are close to you or far away. You and you alone hold the truth. The dog that I am may bark, but Your Excellency's caravan will continue to move on over the inert bodies of the ignorant majority. I promise you that this reason almost eclipsed my desire to speak. Other less important reasons (according to a rather arbitrary set of criteria) prevent critical thoughts from surfacing, and I have reflected on this. All those who have dared to utter a word contrary to praise in this country are in prison, exile, or six feet under. It is more serious than simply being for or against. How many of your fiercest critics from years past are now on your side, their bellies full of the venomous words you made them swallow by bribing them with billions of our precious francs?

But whatever the reasons for remaining silent, Your Excellency, they ultimately carry little weight compared to the afflictions that are ravaging our country: anger (too much violence), envy (too much hatred), avarice (too many hidden treasures), lust (too many celebrations), sloth (too much easy money), pride (too much praise), gluttony (too many stolen billions). Under your leadership, these afflictions have been elevated to cardinal virtues. Virtues to which I would gladly add nepotism, megalomania, constitutional banditry and impunity, careerism, cronyism, incompetence, lies, betrayal, blackmail, murder, corruption, and so on.

This has transformed our country into a kind of gigantic political pandemonium where patriotism and duty are synonymous with anger and public disorder. Pretending to ignore what is happening in our country is no longer an option, and my desire to address you stems from the moral responsibility I feel towards my homeland. You can well imagine, then, that personal considerations will not hold me back. Between you and me, what is at stake goes far beyond our fleeting destinies.

So, as I pick up my pen, only one thing matters to me: telling you the truth that I was referring to. The truth of your people. Of my people. This truth that you dislike, that has the prodigious power of making man immune to fear and despair. I tell you this because I know that, in one way or another, you will respond to this letter. You are not in the habit of letting a crime of lèse-majesté go unpunished. But I am confident that the truth I hold gives me an advantage over you. If you decide to punish me, know that I am prepared to endure whatever you throw my way. If, instead, you feel the urge to buy me off, then I call upon the country, the continent, the world, to witness that I will not play that game.

You have a reputation for putting a price tag on friendship, but you will not have mine. Not in this way. Friendship is only meaningful when it is freely given, which is its most profound expression. But with you, nothing is free.

Even if it were, I believe that any friendship you offer me should also extend to the multitude. So, know this, Mr. President, and I swear it before God: I will not take any of your millions, I will not stay in any of your palaces, I will not feed at any of your troughs. And if, in your great benevolence, you find me worthy of the nation's gratitude (yes, you are capable of that) and decide to reward me in cold hard cash, I authorize you to build a clinic, a classroom, or a movie theater—wherever the cries of people yearning for a better life still haunt the opulent gardens of your dignitaries.

I would also like to tell you that I am not waiting for you to take up your finest pen to reply. Just know, Your Excellency, that it will be difficult for you to cloak yourself in indifference, even though I know you will not. My words demand a response. If, despite my predictions, you feign ignorance, history will once again record that a complaint has risen to reach you, calling you to amend your ways, and that you, certain of your own Omnipotence, have done nothing.

Some intellectuals who are well known in the halls of the capital dissuaded me from writing to you. Do they still deserve that title? Those who long ago gave up risking their necks on the altar of bold criticism, who have appointed themselves "rationalizers" of the order you established, who, in the name of fear, tranquility, or privilege, raise a cowardly veil over your government instead of confronting the absurdity of your rule. Truthfully, I cannot judge that. But when they try to make me complicit in their guilty silence, or worse, when they suggest I join them in their ignoble buffoonery of making the unacceptable acceptable, I tell them "No!" What kind of intellectual refuses to put into words the experience of the majority still suffering under the yoke of tyranny? Are they just a figure locked in an ivory tower, endlessly reasoning without once questioning the blood-soaked petals that grow all around that tower? Even if I would not deny that privilege to the artist, I must note that on the burning lands of Africa—lands boiling with wild rage and a freedom too long suppressed—singing about the beauty of the flamboyant trees is an exorbitant luxury. A justified and even valuable luxury, as long as it demonstrates independence from censorship, but a guilty luxury when speech cannot circulate freely. My conviction is that, while the artist is free to navigate between being, seeming, and not-being, between the pain and the lightness of intimate vision, this freedom loses its meaning when it is feigned. If the alternative is self-censorship and corruption, then the intellectual is forced to get his hands dirty in the swamp of moral depravity. In truth, we cannot continue to shout ourselves hoarse about who we are simply to denounce the Hegelian fallacy and prove that the tabula rasa is a lie. We can no longer celebrate a different Africa, suspended in time, contemplative, and imbued with the innocence of early life. This is how you like your defenders of our culture. While they toil away to uphold an authenticity built on empty words and future promises, you, with complete impunity, plow the aching slopes of our land for the benefit of your clan. These intellectuals, lords of festivals and literary cafés—so susceptible to accolades that they have lost their sense of proportion—should know that the champagne they enjoy in Paris or Stockholm will taste of blood as long as they refuse to open their eyes to our suffering. Until they are willing to put their own personal safety on the line for the advancement of knowledge and the liberation of life, they will remain nothing more than sad clowns, beholden to those who watch with benevolence as you massacre the very reason for your people's existence. To speak of governance in Africa is to literally open the wound, to wash it, and to cauterize it. It is to attack the affliction with more pain. And the immediacy of the pain is commensurate with the urgency of the reaction. It matters little if our dirty laundry is aired in the public square. I would rather aspire to follow in the footsteps of those who understand that truth-telling is inevitable. Those who want to speak their own truth, even if it is subjective, because they refuse to be satisfied with the truth of others. Those truth-tellers who abandon the tone of propriety, magnificent embodiments of the pebble of impertinence in the corrupt sandal of power. Those who are willing to tell it like it is, no matter the circumstances. Those who, whether from here or elsewhere, keep the flame of freedom burning without contempt or condescension, pretension or certainty. These truth tellers know they will not be criticized for meddling in what doesn't concern them or accused of speaking on behalf of a suffering nation, because they are in the same predicament. I prefer to identify with the truth tellers, rather than with your sycophants, your plutocrats, your "evil grigri," your "bedbug of a petty monk," * who demand I be silent. I will not be silent. My voice is that of resistance, my words are the same as those spoken by a man several centuries ago, just a little further south of our country. In a letter like this one, written from the depths of a prison cell where he awaited death for defying authority, he said: "Even if I am beaten to death, I will not be silent, because I am an African." *Ich bin ein Afrikaner!* His name was Estienne Barbier. He was an adventurer, a thief, a bandit, and a rebel. But he was African. He had this profound awareness of belonging to a land that deserves so much more than what it has received so far. A land whose grandeur our entire lives cannot possibly express. We are ready to die for this land.

However, I have neither the soul of a hero nor the makings of a martyr. But Mr. President, there comes a time when

* Translator's Note: "*Mauvais gris-gris*" and "*punaise de moinillon*" were terms first used by Aimé Césaire in his book *Cahiers d'un retour au pay natal.* [Transl. by Eshleman & Smith: *Notebook of a Return to the Native Land*].

the obligation to truth and the passion for one's land intertwine with the courage to exist within it and for it. The most immediate result of this alliance is an immunity to any form of pressure and a firm will to put one's heart and soul into the service of words. I am not saying that I have a superior understanding of Good and Evil. Deep down, I do not believe that one can definitively determine what Good and Evil truly are. But, Mr. President, I love my country with a visceral, unconditional, fierce, and incandescent love. The kind of love that makes a man ready to risk his peace and his life and—God knows how much I love life—to risk everything so that his country remains standing. And when I speak of my country, I speak of myself, I speak of you, I speak of our Africa.

This country deserves to have its dignity restored. Not mine, much less yours, but that of this fragment of African land which has suffered from neglect for far too long, as if it has no other destiny. It is time to tell you bluntly: through unjustifiable arrogance and selfishness, you have betrayed this country and the pact that binds you to it. Seeing you suck the blood of your fellow citizens like a thirsty vampire, watching you rule over them as if they were a court and you a petty, capricious, and narcissistic king, I am compelled, Mr. President, to stand in your way despite my own smallness, despite the insignificant reach of my words. I do this in the name of our shared future. And beware, Mr.

President, because a frail little swallow singing the truth of its people can shake the foundations of a kingdom you wrongly believe to be eternal. The revolt born of its song can make the colossus of your being dissolve like a wax statue under the relentless rays of a new sun. I am not that swallow. It lives within every citizen whose lament rises, almost inaudibly, from homes draped in poverty. It lives within every man and woman of this nation whose voice is ignored and whose flesh is corroding below deck while you are at the helm, bellowing commands to your cabin boys aboard this ship of indifference. It lives within the youth of our country: the youth of the streets, the youth of the ghettos, the youth of the slums, the youth of the boondocks, the youth of the underworld, whose horizon is clouded and whose anger grows like the swell of a tsunami: muffled, deep, tenacious, and irremediable. These bodies, trampled underfoot for so long, are forming into a wave that no armed force, no marabout's protection, and no fortress can withstand. If you do not evacuate, it will soon sweep you away, as it has swept away so many of your predecessors in Africa, into the trenches of collective memory. ▪

LETTER TWO

Mr. President,

I heard you take a stand against the coup d'état with our northern neighbor. It was a halfhearted condemnation, done merely on principle, to hedge your bets and not interfere in the internal affairs of a sister country. Fair enough. Consequently, I would like to discuss with you the methods of securing and maintaining political power that you, as a dissident, had fiercely denounced *urbi et orbi*. Now, as an esteemed member of the brotherhood of democratically elected heads of state, your criticisms are lukewarm at best. These antipodal political stances are clearly not so different from each other in your case.

Don't take this personally, but we can safely bet that all the dictators that rise up in our part of the world are cast from the same mold. Since the celebrated but incomplete declarations of independence, we have witnessed the same recycled tactics of seizing the throne and trampling our fellow citizens to get there—weapons, rigged elections, doctored constitutions, forced successions. Democratic transitions are ultimately so rare and fragile that it's best not to invite bad luck by mentioning them here.

There was a time when we spoke of comic opera generals, ubuesque officers, and cohorts of Caligulas in fatigues who infested African history like ticks on a lion's scrotum. Far, far too many African leaders had blood on their hands. At the turn of the twenty-first century, we were convinced that a new leaf had turned and that these Papa Dictators, these clownish replacements, these heirs of the colonizers would no longer haunt the nights of our new and finally free republics. We swelled with pride and thanked God as the rumble of tanks and the crack of machine guns finally receded from the halls of power. Some of us, though admittedly few, could even boast of never having witnessed the parade of uniforms beneath the pillars of the republic. Then the putsches resumed. As I write these lines, no nation's security, not even our own, is safe from the threat of deranged soldiers. Perhaps these same soldiers who are eyeing your throne while polishing their Kalashnikovs in the dark of the barracks are more numerous than you think.

One is ultimately tempted to believe that coups d'état, armed rebellions, and violent uprisings are the only ways to remove an African head of state—an apparent proof of our incapacity to renounce violence, or for some, of an atavistic brutality that supposedly defines us. We are tired of being represented in this way. I don't know about you, Mr. President, but for me, it is deeply painful to hear that what we are experiencing in Africa is the result of centuries of dehumanization that allows us to shamelessly litter the steps leading to our seats of power with the corpses of people who look like us. People will always say, to muddy the waters, that no, of course Africa does not hold a monopoly on violence; that the conquest and preservation of power have always and everywhere been linked to the need to remove obstacles, even human ones, whatever the price. Whoever is not ready to kill cannot aspire to remain in power. But the truth, sir, is that almost everywhere in the world, mass murder and genocide are becoming increasingly intolerable, and all societies have enshrined the sanctity of life as a non-negotiable value. How painful it is to know that our lives mean so little in the eyes of the world. It hurts terribly, Mr. President. And you, back home, far from being moved by our plight, continue to play games with our lives.

Certainly, the figure of the Father of the Nation is a thing of the past. Are a charismatic young captain and self-designated patriotic officers the best option for our people as our hopes and dreams are endlessly postponed? A dictator doesn't ever truly change; he is just recycled. The novelty now is to brandish the idea of a democratic transition, promise elections that will take place immediately and, when the time comes, quietly manipulate the results with the expertise of one's peers, who are masters in the art of defying the laws of arithmetic. To stay in power, the new strongman—or better yet, the transitional committee—need only rely on a circle of cronies who use their connections to sidle up to the major neocolonial powers. With a little luck and a few strategic bribes, especially if the predecessor had fallen from grace, the job is done. Once the European Union and the United States give their stamp of approval, then they're open for business. The African Union and the regional organizations will finish the job and christen the new regime with African-style accolades: bump me on the forehead, pat me on the back, and I will protect you.

When the consent of the white colonizer is absent, extensive manipulation tactics and intense negotiations will be required to reassure the Empire that its voracious appetite for raw materials will continue to be satiated. This step is essential. Then, it will suffice to mitigate any disruption from the press, the courts, civil society, and what's left of already moribund institutions. Even more convenient to have docile people who put up no resistance, out of fear, fatalism, or both. Once power is secured, the price of certain commodities is lowered, and Caesar's promises are made to those who believe, the people will return to their peaceful, pathetic acceptance of servitude. The Society of Control sets up shop, more or less indefinitely. Until the next coup, that is. Then the plundering can begin, with the gradual implementation of a reticulated system of embezzlement that has proven its effectiveness over time. Everyone, except those who are hungry, benefits from it. Members of the inner circle become powerful, while the Western friends of the former head of state blithely switch allegiances and provide information on the nebulous network of offshore accounts in tax havens, arms deals, esoteric protections systems, and strategic alliances.

It sometimes happens that these Western friends back out. Either the deal doesn't quite suit them, or China and Russia gladly invite themselves to the party. In this case, human rights violations and the imperatives of the transfer of power suddenly become urgent matters. As threats of boycotts and bans crystallize, every African president must now learn the intricacies of propaganda and mass manipulation in order to respond effectively on the battlefield of communication. But on a continent still searching for a positive role model, there may be some benefit to being the troublemaker and opposing the old masters. This new trend is beginning to touch the hearts of many. Amid the decolonial fervor, the goal is to embody as best as possible the desire of all Africans to liberate themselves from the demons of imperialism. With these hand-me-down Cold

War ideologies continuing to feed and distort geopolitics, it is in good form to align with so-called anti-imperialist powers that, in reality, dream of setting up shop in Africa. After all, France, Great Britain, and the United States have embodied Satan with so much conviction that one can sell one's people to a Mammon or a Beelzebub while passing for Thomas Sankara. What a cruel step backward.

I grew up in a time when any person with a gun could position themselves as a freedom fighter. Has anything truly changed since then? How could it be possible if freedom is always beholden to military control? I bear no hatred towards soldiers. I mistrust them. Just like you. How, then, can we protect ourselves from their incursions into the shifting sands of politics? By using transparency and the ephemeral nature of power to one's advantage. That alone would render futile the military's attempts to seize control. Otherwise, they will have no trouble discrediting people like you to legitimize their own power grabs.

Today, the sacred texts have replaced the Marxist handbook, but it would only take a few lucky allies, a few contracts for gold, diamonds, or oil, some modest shipments of weapons that will gradually increase, and a few ragged vigilantes to launch the assault of capitals and presidential palaces. The same revolutionary groups, which are as disorganized as ever and as ill-equipped as the regular army, are still capable of launching an insurrection at any moment.

Rebellion is a breeding ground for the imagination, releasing a carnival of horrors in its wake. Behind these amateur killers lurk the same pathetic nobodies in tracksuits, just as likely to take their inspiration from God as from Pamela Anderson. Each one with the conviction that they possess both power and truth. They strut around under the influence of indoctrination experts who can transform any belief into a cause worthy of mass destruction. To achieve these goals, one must be prepared to kill or be killed. Preferably to kill. Ethnicity, religion, and land have a greater sacred value than before. Criminalized teenagers patiently carry out the dirty work. These thrilling missions give them a sense of purpose—something they were deprived of in their previously idle and mundane lives. Unfortunately, many young Africans are easily manipulated by promises of liberation. And a silent, irrational violence lies dormant in the hearts of these youth, who have been nurtured on anger and frustration. The tribute that these people pay to these defenders of the lumpenproletariat generation, armed with useless diplomas, unattainable dreams, action movies, the internet, drugs, the Bible or the Quran, is immeasurable. As I write this, towns and villages are being burned, innocent people are being horribly mutilated, spiritual and intellectual leaders are being shamefully assassinated, and entire populations are being massacred. All in the name of the struggle inspired by the defenders, or rather, the *entrepreneurs* of African dignity.

What dignity? The dignity stolen from women and children who, in reality, bear the brunt of the insanity from these dealers of hatred. Wives, mothers, cousins, sisters—sometimes barely past puberty—are beaten and raped in the name of restoring this supposed African dignity. Imagine, Mr. President, the cold metal of canons in these women's privates, their breasts ripped from them, their modest loincloths undone in the dark night of the Revolution. Imagine the rapes that accompany the promise of liberty. What fate awaits these women and their children—the young seeds of our future? We have seen people play soccer with the heads of newborns or smash them against palm trees. We have seen little girls suffer the torment of revolutionary marriages. We have seen so many helpless bodies fall victim to short-term gains. Sometimes, the desire for ultimate power uses the flesh and blood of innocent people, our blood, in cannibalistic banquets intended to protect our executioners from their own demise and prolong their control over us.

You cannot pretend you have no hand in what is happening to these defenseless beings who are humiliated and deprived of their humanity, with no refuge other than silence. The people who best represent the vulnerability of Africa are those who are never invited to discussions about the future of the nation. The continent of Africa is merely a chessboard for the ambitions of others; its own children reduced to pawns in the hands of criminals. Ultimately, both perpetrators and victims have lost their dignity as a result, and the name of Africa will forever be associated with this tragedy.

Tell me, Mr. President, have you considered ways to end this massacre? Are you familiar with the curse of the giant who has all the food in the world and yet still insists on devouring his own flesh? Ultimately, some ask, what's wrong with eliminating lives that we just can't sustain? The burden of Africa's population is a convenient excuse for those who allow massacres to take place in the name of Malthusianist ideology. They use biopolitics as a tool to manage the lives of the working class and have convinced you that you can never kill too many Africans. They forget that the lives that serve the interests of the great capital are just as valuable as the lives that do not. Mouths to feed are no less precious than muscles to exploit, for both are sustained by the same breath of life. When your fellow Heads of State demand respect for the lives of their own people while reducing yours to an economic variable, they force you to renounce your humanity. The life of an African is worth more than a corrupt suitcase of cash. Everyone knows it. No one shows it.

I can barely scratch the surface of the potential ramifications of this parallel between power and violence, for they are infinite. In principle, seizing power through violence, however it manifests itself, is unforgivable. You might counter that there is a fundamental difference between armed bandits and governments that enforce their power through police and military forces. You might even say it's outrageous to compare African countries to some kind of lawless Wild West ravaged by instability. But tell me, sir, what would you call a country whose police are quick to arrest anyone who utters even the subtlest word of dissent? What would you call a country whose justice system is under orders to snuff out even the slightest hint of protest? A place where thugs mercilessly harass and beat anyone who complains? How would you describe a nation where the righteous are murdered, and children, virgins, albinos, and disabled people are sacrificed on the altar of power? What does a country stand for when ex-officials are imprisoned, opponents are terrorized, and intellectuals are eliminated or exiled? Different actors, same script.

You, sir, have neither staged a military coup nor used armed conflict to gain power. But does that automatically mean you are innocent? All your despicable acts bring you closer to the people I just described, not further from them. It seems like you boast to your peers about being a fervent defender of human rights, and you manage to convince your allies that any violations made by the opposition in our country are pure fabrications. At worst, you would condone the use of force to guarantee the order and safety of your citizens. For you, safety comes at the price of blood. The blood that you refuse to see on your hands is what brings you closest to the Devil.

You have been accused of many things. Regardless of which of these horrors you have or have not committed, from my point of view, you are guilty of them all as long as you refuse to devote yourself to making this country safer for all citizens no matter their place of residence, their ethnic background, or their political affiliation. Regardless of the circumstances, these people died in our country because of politics. We are talking about murder, Mr. President. Until these deaths are brought justly and completely to light, you are responsible for them. No envelope delivered to families of victims and no national tribute will change that. I would go so far as to say, Mr. President, that every murder committed in our country can be directly attributed to you, and the victims will continue to turn in their graves as long as they are not given the justice they deserve. I would like you to remember this, you and all the heads of state in Africa and elsewhere who believe only in disposing of all political obstacles.

And we endure another form of violence, more insidious and perverse, that you and your supporters dismiss. This violence is of a symbolic, psychological, and moral nature, and prevents us, in all circumstances, from reaching our full potential. Mr. President, political violence does not need to be open and direct to be denounced. I would like you to know that the violence I am referring to takes many forms, and what matters more than its form is the human being it affects. Harming a person's psychological integrity is just as detestable as harming their physical integrity. And in our country, we are victims of a great deal of emotional violence.

We have lost all faith in ourselves and all hope in our future. This is primarily because you have never allowed us to live with confidence in our abilities. It is said that people only get the leaders they deserve. I am quite conflicted about such an assertion. You have manipulated these people with the complicity of the religious establishment and imposed the idea that they could give up their basic human rights in the hope of a brighter future.

Before closing, Your Excellency, I would like to share a dream I had. In my dream, I saw a country whose citizens went to the polls to elect their representatives in peace and transparency. I saw a country where masses could vote to exercise their freedom when their leader did not deliver. I saw a country where neither the government's credibility nor its longevity depended on Western chancelleries. A country in which foreign conglomerates did not dare to meddle in political affairs. A country where political debate was not tainted by partisan interests. A country where unlimited terms of office were an aberration and a lifelong presidency was insanity. That country is not mine. Not yet.

I would like to see this country move towards peace. But if it takes an earthquake, so be it. This "whatever it takes" mentality among your neighbors is what precipitated the rise of the young captain who frightens you so much. It is the ultimate paradox of our condition to want today what we abhorred yesterday. We have come to realize that the uniform does not make the man. Perhaps these recurring coups will simply stir up change, not freedom. What a terrible admission of powerlessness. I will never be convinced that force is a reasonable political recourse. Meanwhile, you and your ilk have turned the political chessboard into a battlefield where anything goes. Take some moral responsibility. We are tired. ▪

LETTER THREE

Mr. President,

I live in a small village that you have never set foot in. Do you think you might someday? Only if oil were discovered there, or a diamond mine, or who knows what. Your Excellency only travels to remote corners when a higher interest demands it. Yet, in speech after speech, you invite our fellow citizens to discover the treasures of our land. Have you ever stayed in a small, rural tourist establishment? If you and your officials had been willing to promote this idea of local holidays, imagine the impact it would have had on domestic tourism. Instead, your few visits to the provinces have mainly served to line the pockets of your friends who own large hotels in each region.

The upcoming local elections won't be enough to add our humble town to your mental map, but we learned the other day that you've given your blessing to your Minister of Rivers and Artificial Lakes as a candidate in the mayoral race. Once the initial surprise wore off, we tried to figure out why you made such a choice, since we had never heard of this person before this year, nor of the Ministry of Rivers and Artificial Lakes. It's not that we're out of touch with the realities of our country, but like almost everyone else, we've lost track of who does what in your government.

It must be said that, to accommodate your political clientele, you've mastered the art of pulling the most improbable ministries and agencies out of your hat. There is an absurdity here that only you and your African peers can explain. I personally know people who, not long ago, were struggling to make ends meet. Today, they are completely out of touch with the impoverished neighborhoods where they grew up. Gone are the family homes, the squalid apartments, the broken down junkers; replaced with palaces, luxury cars, and country estates. The nouveaux riches know no limits. If only it were worth it. At your command, men and women with no training or qualifications parade their amateurism for all to see. Every Wednesday, without fail, you present us with a complete overhaul of the State apparatus. Each day brings its share of upstarts who drain our meager resources and gorge themselves, knowing that they can bail out at any moment.

We're all too familiar with the cumbersome nature of government bureaucracy. Just look at the operating budgets of our ministries, the national directorates of this, the regional offices of that. We are a poor, resourceless country, specialized in recycling political parasites and white-collar crooks. The fewer resources we have, the more numerous our government officials become, despite your promises of austerity. My mother used to say that a herd of horses, no matter how richly harnessed, cannot guarantee victory if ridden into battle by mediocre cavalrymen. She didn't know you yet. Still, to your credit, it must be said that the entire country seems averse to simplicity, pragmatism, and humility. Let's not forget that "I don't care" has always been our motto. Walk into any government office and you'll see the proof. But there's no point in hoping for change in the political sphere when the entire country is plagued by the same curse. It's what keeps you in power; naturally, you're not trying to change the situation. I have always found astonishing the mediocrity in which the civil service wallows, and which bureaucrats mindlessly perpetuate. It's as if working for our country somehow robs us of any desire to do good work. Who among us hasn't faced the obstacle course of navigating the bureaucratic jungle? Who hasn't cursed the mess that passes for the civil service in this country? Sometimes, a case can be stalled indefinitely over a simple signature. One missing detail is enough to paralyze an entire administration. One absence . . .

Ultimately, your management of our country's human and economic resources perfectly reflects the huge mess we're living in: a large and poorly trained workforce, ignorant and arrogant staff, absent decision-makers. Is this the cause or consequence of bad governance? Who knows? I am no longer outraged when I see offices filled with idle bureaucrats, air conditioners and TVs blaring, endless breakfasts, stacks of neglected files, official vehicles turned into shopping cars used to deliver personal packages—these are not local supermarkets, I'm talking about administrative offices where unchecked bedlam is continuously spreading.

I myself am a product of this system, I don't deny it. But that doesn't stop me from seeing that it's flawed. I went to college, I earned my degrees, and yet I didn't have to struggle to find a job. Perhaps because I haven't really been trained in anything. I heard a politician say that this country doesn't train enough scientists and professionals. That makes me smile a little when I look at our scientists and professionals. The education system has other problems. The first vocation we need to teach our children is excellence.

There was a time when none of this bothered me because I live in a small village that I used to think was relatively safe. We were very aware that our destinies were tied to the land that nourished us. But today, the danger is real, of transforming our ancient environment into a large shopping mall against our will. You, the politicians, have failed to sow the seeds of revolution and true African independence. You have turned us into docile consumers: the last links in a chain of globalization whose beneficiaries are the producers, not the consumers. We have everything, we work poorly, we consume excessively—a sad assessment of our modernity.

I'm straying a bit from the reason for this letter. I wanted to talk to you about my village. We understand why our small community of a few hundred souls has suddenly become the object you covet. And I tell you, Mr. President, I would much prefer our village had no mineral resources at all so we could preserve the peace and quiet we've enjoyed all these years. Mind you, we're not against progress. We have simply learned by observing what happens in other nations: in Africa, the promise of urbanization systematically coincides with the onset of a social, economic, and environmental curse. And the discovery of mineral wealth has only provided us with a blueprint for our decline. So, for us, cultivating our land, grazing our animals, and keeping our forests pristine is how we escape the absurdity of commercial modernity, which, in reality, is simply an attempt to erase a living ecosystem. By rejecting this idea of modernity, which reduces human beings to the value of their possessions, we reflect a greater desire to preserve seeds for the future. The seeds of life must be preserved, Mr. President. They are the vessel of our humanity.

We are afflicted by constant fears. For centuries, our soil has been steadily nourished by minerals that seem to have transformed overnight into a treasure that will set us permanently on a path to industrialization. Experts have come to inform us that beneath our village beach lies an abundance of these valuable minerals, which apparently have endless uses for the automotive, technology, aerospace, luxury, and pharmaceutical sectors—and many others that don't even exist here. And so, I'll say this plainly: by calling for its exploitation, you are giving us the kiss of death. This country was rich in nothing, but at least that nothing brought us peace. You must understand that these minerals, which have brought new wealth to southern lands, will bring about our ruin even before the ravenous West finishes extracting them from our mines. They have already planned to cut down the flamboyant trees, raze the mangroves, dig up the entire village, and lay waste to the coastline without even bothering to consult us first. It's true that negotiations are taking place at government headquarters in the capital. Your experts don't seem to care much about what the people here think. It's more of a technical issue than an ethical one.

We have only our land, our rice paddies, and this sandbar that protects them. Water threatens this precarious balance as it slowly and inexorably erodes the sand. The dune here is weeping, like every other place where the almighty power of money has dictated its fate. A world already battered by the jealous ocean, but still alive, has now been handed its death sentence. Nature is dying—no more mangroves, no more crabs, no more grey herons. Every living thing is being consumed by Your Majesty's insatiable appetite.

Mr. President, do you know what real progress is? It is when dreaming is not a luxury but a choice. It is when we can eat our fill, heal ourselves in our own gardens, marvel at life's miracles, and even learn and transmit the secrets of the life force that animates us. This is what has ensured the resilience of our people. This is what has brought happiness to our lives. We did not fear for the future when the will of our gods was at the heart of human endeavors. This forest you see here is the temple of those gods. We have always sanctified every grove, venerated every breath of life in this space. We have hidden life in every tuft of grass. That is why all the money in the world will never hold the slightest appeal for us. But when I look at your past, I realize that we don't have the same vision of what a modern country should be.

You are said to be the spearhead of major projects: the builder. You are the one we must thank for supposedly launching our country into an era of progress with your pharaonic achievements, your roads, your statues, your monuments, your infrastructures. Paradoxically, I have a feeling that these achievements will not go down in history. You have transformed our capital overnight and now it is beginning to look like a mid-sized Western city. Bravo. But let me tell you a story. One of my many cousins from the north, whom you made wealthy, invited some Western friends to visit his new house built in one of the capital's upscale neighborhoods. When they arrived, he showed off his electronic sliding gate, his security cameras, his modern plumbing system, his indoor swimming pool, his two living rooms with automated lighting and AC, his indoor elevators, his marble bathtubs. The same man who just a few years ago had been renting an apartment in his provincial town, had made it big. He told them about other villas belonging to government officials that rivaled his in luxury and gadgetry. Real smart homes, he said. But his guests, who had come to sign a mining contract, were not at all impressed. Later, these same friends came to our village and, chatting among themselves right here in front of us, were openly amused by my cousin's pride in his new acquisitions, not thinking for a moment that we could understand what they were saying. They went on to make fun of our people, who were dying of poverty, and thought only of luxury and superficial things. What my cousin didn't know, what he should have known, was that most of the amenities he boasted of were in fact standard conveniences in any Western house. He didn't know that his visitors had seen plenty of smart homes around the world before coming to Africa, and that instead of earning their respect, he had made a fool of himself in their eyes.

What is the connection, you might ask? Well, Mr. President, your efforts to "modernize" our country remind me of my cousin's efforts to turn his house into a palace. It's certainly commendable, but if we think we can impress the world by filling our country with gadgets, we're sorely mistaken, because in other places, these gadgets are as commonplace as they are useful. A foreigner arriving in our country, unless still infected by colonial prejudices, will not be surprised to find an ultramodern airport and four-lane highway in our capital, nor shocked to land on a rural airstrip and then take a bush taxi to their hotel. In both cases, it would be foolish to make a big deal out of it when everyone knows that the level of economic power is not the same between Africa and the West, and that the former cannot progress any faster or slower than its current circumstances allow.

The usefulness of infrastructure does not lie in its ability to dazzle visitors. It is useful only when it is part of a robust human development program. And Mr. President, those of us who have traveled have seen that people elsewhere are selling their cars and opting for bikes instead. It seems they also want to go plastic-free, eat organic food, create urban farms, and depollute their cities. In a way, they're trying to adopt *our* way of life. The elevator that you wanted us to take to join them at the top is the same one they're taking back down to earth.

As I see it, the billions you're pouring into the capital's highways would have been better spent on sub-regional transportation and communication networks and building roads to connect to the interior of the country. Just like constructing several bridges between Kinshasa and Brazzaville would be a more relevant project than a five-star hotel in Khartoum, an ultra-modern convention center in Bissau, or a high-tech football stadium in Djibouti. It's as basic as prioritizing social needs. If you must build something, make sure it is part of a genuine and relevant socio-economic consideration. And if all of this effort is ultimately just about your own vanity and obsession with a modern-looking Africa, then it's about as impressive as installing a speed trap in the Kalahari Desert.

There has been much talk of your plan to build a monument to Africa because you saw one while visiting a neighboring country—a country whose president is well-known for his megalomaniacal delusions. Is this really someone you want to emulate? The completion of this project has only reinforced your astounding ability to turn gold into lead. From the moment it was announced, it set tongues wagging in households across the country. Your opponents, who love nothing more than to drag you through the mud, took advantage of the situation to belittle the idea and try to nip it in the bud. No use. The people also surprised you by rejecting your "masonic and pagan" monument with such vehemence that, as usual, it was necessary to use a carrot-and-stick approach to get them to accept the plan. It has become anachronistic to protest against this monument and timelier to reflect on how to prevent it from becoming just another forgotten whim of a capricious President. You missed this opportunity. Personally, I liked the idea more than its execution, and I'll tell you why.

Let's agree that this monument, through a series of errors, demonstrated the government's negligence and incompetence in project management. The first error was related to the vision of the project itself. To begin with, I do not believe the name—*Monument of Emergence and Liberation*—was truly appropriate since the liberation of Africa had been decreed with the granting of independence. And if there was anything that could appropriately symbolize this event, it would be a monument to those who died for independence. Let's move on.

The mark of a true builder is to involve all sectors of their people in projects of this magnitude. For this project, however, you put your name on the base of the monument before it even rose from the ground, relegating your fellow citizens to the role of mere observers. One does not declare oneself a great helmsman by engraving one's name on a pediment. It is history and the collective conscience that connect our names to achievements that have marked our passage. No matter what you say, you also gave this structure a value that is more touristic than revolutionary or educational. In this regard, I am not convinced patriotism is at the heart of the idea.

I have also wondered about the secretive nature of your approach. There should have been a structure, a council bringing together artists, intellectuals, engineers, and local elected officials, formally appointed to gather the most relevant opinions and share them with the public. Instead, you decided everything in closed-door meetings with your friends, often irrationally—which explains the abrupt reversals, budget overruns, postponements, and cancellations. A timeline should have been established, and proof of the project's financial viability should have been made public. Before discussing profits, a full reimbursement to the public treasury of the sums invested in these colossal works should have been considered, and only then should operational costs be addressed. This would have been more dignified than trying to explain to the public that this building cost them nothing and hoping they would believe you simply because you said so. Does this mean that your word is worth more than their capacity to understand? It is a grave mistake to think that governing a nation also means governing its thoughts. We gave you the helm to do what is good for the people, not to dictate it to them.

Throughout your term, you have never stopped building, which is good. Very good, even. But this monument was one project too many, in that you imposed it as your own personal achievement despite all opposition. For this construction project, you went so far as to deliberately threaten the fragile economic balance and social stability of a country as poor as ours. This monument symbolizes a political rule marked by caprice and voracity. You don't seem to understand the profoundly symbolic value of the presidential signature. If a signature is a trivial tool used to validate the whims of one man, it is because the conscience of its holder is as absent as his vision. Abuses like this have justified accusations of despotism, dictatorship, and who knows what else—your unilateral decisions apply equally to all sectors of the administration. We would be no less excluded, even without parliament, civil society, or political opposition.

So, we are the republic of ostentation and money. You love that word so much that I would be remiss not to mention it. Cold hard cash! The Alpha and Omega of your reign. Why this irrational love for money? You have taken so much, given so much. What need do you have for these unlimited funds (called "political funds" by some and "slush funds" by others), that you apparently use as you please? You have corrupted the entire country, and no words can bring you back to your senses. For over a decade, suitcases full of cash have been flying around like spaceships in Stars Wars. How can you explain, in a country as poor as ours, the indecent salaries you have granted, the bribes, the per diems, the unlimited fees? How do you justify taking a private jet to go on a shopping spree in Geneva, or keeping luxury cars parked in palaces, or booking out entire cruise ships? How can you forgive proven embezzlement, the plundering of public funds, and unexplained sales of property belonging to the State? What do you have to say about the accusations against your family? Why do you remain silent, Mr. President? Do you need to amass so much wealth when you know how fleeting life is? When I see and hear about everything you have willingly done in the name of money, I cannot find a shred of rationality in your mind. Yet it is this very mind that embodies the face of our nation. Maybe one day we will understand your appetite for material wealth.

In the meantime, Mr. President, let me say this to you: the man you are sending to govern our village is certainly like you, but we are not like him. We do not want outsiders showing up on our doorstep to tell us how to live. We simply want leaders who know how to help us live better lives. If that doesn't seem reasonable to you, let us live like nobodies while you continue transforming the country for those who cling to gold and machinery. As for us, we prefer to hold onto the seeds. ▪

LETTER FOUR

Mr. President,

This is the fourth letter I am sending you. I wonder if you are beginning to enjoy this one-way correspondence as much as you seem to enjoy having the exclusive right to speak. I am naïve enough to think that you might learn a few things from our time together. This may come as a surprise, but I see a parallel in our antithetical lives. In truth, our destinies are so intertwined that it's as if our two lives are one. I'll concede that I possess fewer human virtues than you. This is precisely why I quickly developed an aversion to positions of responsibility. It's not for lack of charisma or charm—the people closest to me often tell me that I am cut from the same cloth as the greats of the world. A friend of mine, whom you also know, told me, "It's too easy to criticize the political actions of our leaders from where you're sitting. Politics belongs to no one. If you have ideas and a sense of duty, there is no reason to lecture others from your armchair. If you do that, the vultures will always have free rein to continue their dirty work. It's certainly risky to get involved in politics in Africa, but the people demand it as long as our hands are clean." That friend is now one of the men who disturbs your sleep. May he stay alive!

Personally, I decided long ago to avoid political leadership in any form, even locally in my own village, because of my deep conviction that politics should be synonymous with exemplarity. Well aware of the baggage I carry in my own modest existence, I have always been careful—beyond my close confidants—not to tell others which path they ought to follow. I have never claimed to be better than anyone else. As such, I cannot imagine claiming responsibility for a project that affects an entire nation. You can see, then, why I am fascinated by you and by your courage to stand before the tribunal of history. At times I wonder whether it is you we should try to understand or our nation, whose values are as asymmetrical as they are protean.

Yesterday, I had a visit from a friend named Ousmane. The name is pure coincidence; please do not read anything into it. I mainly bring this up because we spent a good part of the night discussing politics, as two friends who had not seen each other in thirty years would do. He's an old friend, the kind of friend with whom I appear in time-yellowed photographs featuring younger, slimmer, humbler versions of ourselves. Since you've been a fixture of public life for years, you naturally came up in our conversation. In any case, it was either talk about politics or discuss Marcelo Bielsa's football philosophy. As you know, our people have three passions: sports, politics, and religion, in that order. Seeing as my friend and I were not fans of the Argentine prophet and had already booked our train tickets to hell, the only thing left for us to discuss was politics, if we were going to try to convert each other to the true faith. Although we rarely see eye-to-eye, we were, to my great surprise, quick to agree that you would not be remembered as one of the great figures of our history. And hearing from someone else that you were a poor politician with a weak sense of political timing and about as much charisma as a cassava root made me realize there was no need to harp on about your shortcomings. Although irony and satire are all that remains of our freedom, I myself have little taste for ad hominem attacks.

Our discussion was broader in scope, and we amused ourselves by sketching a sort of composite portrait of the ideal president. We agreed that while it's unrealistic to expect a leader to be superhuman, we are entitled to expect a leader to have certain fundamental qualities. The important thing is not that these qualities come naturally to him, but that he demonstrates them over the course of his term, and that he is capable of rising to a certain level of greatness, befitting of his office. Thus, we conceived of a president who, alas, in our present situation can exist only in the shifting contours of the imagination. It is indeed true that describing a man's qualities is no simple feat—still less so when that man is a public figure, glimpsed only in a pale reflection, altered by the harsh light of power. If I were to assess the qualities of a president, I wouldn't focus on whether he is friendly, funny, quick-tempered, or solitary. I would judge the image of the man by comparing his rhetoric to his public actions. It is not so much about the man as it is about the office. I hope we can agree that a politician does not have to possess all the right qualities to effectively carry out his duty. A great president can be a complete idiot, a weak or arrogant man in his private life, while still demonstrating moral greatness in his political decisions. History has given us many examples of this. The private lives of the greatest figures have always fueled discussions on television, and in lecture halls, train stations, workshops, and bars. In Africa, the correlation between a politician's personal qualities and his office goes beyond mere gossip. It takes on a more serious dimension when power remains vested in the figure of the charismatic leader rather than in a virtuous system built to withstand the faults of any one person.

Today, your character is being compared to that of your political opponents. Unable to burnish your reputation, your supporters have resorted to showing that your opponents aren't exactly saints either. This is the situation we are in. We seek salvation in the virtue of a good man, and yet we fear the human weakness of a leader.

What makes for a good leader? Can we define a good or bad leader without closely examining the inner workings of his power? A public figure, whose actions are judged in the public sphere, conceives of those actions in the privacy of his own conscience. One cannot therefore separate the reality of the subject in the public sphere from his existence in the private one. By trying to focus on a system rather than a person's character, we will inevitably find ourselves evaluating the person who represents the system. It is true that public and private are even more connected in our country where the person and the institution are inseparable. Power is personified in the individual who wields it, and that individual is bound to shine brightly in the spotlight. This is not necessarily the vocation of a head of state. The institution that the president embodies should be as present in our minds as his private reality is in our memory. But as I said, for us, the president isn't just a disembodied figure of power; far from it. He becomes indistinguishable from his office, no matter the situation. He appears everywhere, debating with every person and speaking on every subject. At the end of the day, what seems difficult to me is teasing out authenticity from pantomime in this *mise en abyme* of power. What stems from the sovereignty of the people, and what comes from the depths of a man's character? As such, I leave open the possibility that my judgment of the president might not match up with the reality of the man himself and his character. And I will add that the man's character concerns me very little, because he has not given me enough to properly assess whether his attitudes are consistent with the future role of head of state. I do not want to judge a man based on his limitations. As I said before, great statesmen have proven to be mediocre individuals in their private lives. Thomas Aquinas said it too. The opposite is equally true. Even our moral guides display as much virtue in their speeches as they behave like outright delinquents when the lights go out.

I don't know if you are a good father and loving husband, Mr. President. Instead, let's consider a more general trait that could be unanimously applied to you: political courage. Over the course of your career, you made decisions and choices that alienated you from the previous regime and threatened your freedom. This political courage cost you your freedom and stripped you of your privileges. This does not necessarily mean that you're a courageous man in the truest sense of the word. Those who know you describe you as very attentive to your wife. You're not exactly what we'd call a "real man," despite what your supporters' hagiographies and the political battles you have waged might suggest. Let's be clear, Mr. President. I am not judging your intimate relationship with your wife, nor am I praising machismo. I do think that we should acknowledge the work you've done to promote women in your party, especially in a society where masculinity and patriarchal power are still considered the hallmarks of true leadership. You have made great strides to shift the narrative on this issue. Those who don't appreciate you continue to credit your wife for this achievement, rather than you. If the only thing you were being criticized for was your real or perceived subservience to your wife, I would be the first to defend you. And what goes on behind the closed doors of the Republic is of little concern to me as a citizen anyway.

Any man who aspires to shape the destiny of his fellow citizens has natural strengths and weaknesses, just like everyone else. We cannot judge these in themselves, since objectivity is impossible and circumstances are constantly changing. But we expect this person to enhance their natural strengths and mitigate their shortcomings in the performance of their duties. Your courage as a dissident cannot be compared to your habit of saying "yes, dear" at home. But the problem arises when "yes, dear" extends to buying a villa with public funds. As President, even the smallest personal decision can affect the entire nation. How are you navigating this situation, Mr. President? It seems to me that if a head of state can be courageous in public, he should also be courageous in private. If your decisions fall to your wife or children, then the courage you embody is nothing more than a facade likely to crack at the slightest conflict of interest. If the presidential family was not so involved in public affairs, no one would question your private spinelessness. This blurs the distinction between an individual living their own life and a public body wielding political power. If I were to resort to a metaphor, I would say that public and private life are like two sides of the same coin. What matters most is not the heads side, which would be public life, opposed to the tails side, symbolizing private life, but rather the very material of which the coin is made. The value of the coin is less important than the value of the metal itself. A coin may be identical to others in composition, metal, and weight—but does that mean they are of equal value? Perhaps in the end, the value of these coins does not depend on their weight or on the mint mark they bear, but rather on the system that minted them. I'm framing the issue this way to move beyond your illustrious self—no offense intended. What I am truly trying to determine is what ultimately constitutes the benchmark for judging a leader's abilities. You would certainly appreciate this idea of dissolving the individual into the system. Judging the whole. The government? The state? The people?

Indeed, it is often said that governments reflect the image of their people. Remember, we get the leaders we deserve. If this is true, it would be difficult to condemn you outside of the system that created you. The same friend I mentioned had a clear view on this issue. Here's what he told me: "The current situation in Africa is fundamentally the opposite of that in other continents. So, one of two things must be true. Either Africans do indeed have specific flaws that may be systemic—I do not mean congenital—in which case this would account for the continent's chronic difficulties and the incompetence of those in power, the problem lying at the root; or Africans are no different from other peoples, and one must conclude that for decades, even centuries, they have been victims of the caprice of the gods of politics, condemned by bad fortune to be ruled by leaders who are inept and devoid of worth. In the latter case, I find it impossible to make sense of the fact that this should be the shared experience of every country on the continent, without exception, and that it has persisted for so long."

I am not a proponent of sweeping generalizations, and I made sure to remind him that the so-called "Third World" was not only made up of African countries, and that African countries themselves are at very different levels of development. But we did agree on certain things. Africa is home to some of the most poorly governed countries in the world. And moreover, the differences between African countries are not significant enough to dismiss the idea that the entire continent is politically bankrupt. A common mistake in this situation is seeking out an African leader who can successfully inspire progress, all while neglecting to reflect on our responsibilities as citizens. On the other hand, an honest examination of Africa's political power dynamics would help explain why models that succeed elsewhere fail here. But how can we make a clear assessment if we always put our pride before our responsibility? We should be able to discuss structural or cultural limitations in Africa when talking about politics. Just as we freely discuss the moral corruption of others, their depraved customs, and their idiotic racism, all while forgetting our own. These may be clichés, but they are a good place to start. They allow us to make assumptions that, even when untrue, can still be helpful for further discussion. This list is by no means exhaustive, but I have chosen to highlight a few pitfalls that we must address with urgency and determination.

First, there is the issue of obscurantism. In Africa, the conditions for the emergence of knowledge are nothing short of disastrous, and this alarming phenomenon is what makes your control over us possible. How can we expect to establish a functioning democracy when, for example, a religious leader has free rein to tell a university professor whom he must vote for? How can the same marabout convince an entire country that it is perfectly normal to grant him all kinds of worldly privileges, when half the population lives in poverty and when he himself is supposed to place spiritual life above material concerns? Motivated by these luxuries, many religious men have joined forces with politicians. Clergy that allies itself with corrupt power is just as corrupt. Why must these aberrations be taken for granted? Our governments squander billions maintaining illegitimate favors at the expense of populations who have no say on the matter. We need to first understand these baseless alliances in order to challenge them. We need our own Enlightenement—provided we agree that this Enlightenment is not a dehumanizing borrowing of values that are not ours, but a positive appropriation of our own values and their integration with foreign ones. Many have succeeded in this synthesis. We are the only ones still clinging to false values under the pretext that they are centuries old. And in many cases, this is merely a smokescreen that poorly conceals our ignorance. It seems delusional to expect progress when knowledge is in the hands of so few. Whatever the cost—whatever the language—Africa must build a system of education worthy of the name. This pursuit has many ramifications, but as long as more than sixty percent of our population remains functionally illiterate, we can expect nothing from the future. Some might say that intellectuals are insecure, or worse, that they are digging our country's grave. I would readily agree if we were talking about the kind of comprador bourgeoisie that uses the keys of knowledge to profit from the ignorance of others. This bourgeoisie, beholden to former powers, the Roman Church, or to Arab traditions, has little to do with the system of knowledge transmission that transforms the destiny of a nation. We are situated in the worst possible epistemic configuration because we have rendered knowledge esoteric. Society suffers terrible consequences when those who have access to knowledge lack social intelligence. Knowledge becomes a spider, spinning webs of mass manipulation. I do not believe in a system in which students view the acquisition of knowledge not as a necessity, but rather as a mere favor to society. Do you not also think that the budget allocated to higher education should instead be directed toward primary and early childhood education? It may seem absurd—I myself am not entirely convinced of this approach—but my intuition is telling me that we should be spending more on children to avoid wasting money on adults who were poorly educated from the start and who no longer prioritize the pursuit of knowledge.

The next issue to address is ethnocentrism. And here, I sincerely think that we are still dragging behind us the ball and chain of colonialism. What African can truly claim to know their culture and that of the people around them? We cannot build anything lasting without first respecting our own humanity and that of our neighbors. And the concept of the modern state, inherited from independence movements, has caused us to forget the political realities that existed before. We must understand that colonization is a parenthesis, not the beginning of African history. We must return to dialogue among African peoples, learn to respect one another as Africans, and avoid reproducing racist, essentialist modes of relating. Maybe then we can avoid reproducing racist schema rooted in essentialist relationships. Perhaps the key to unity and peace lies in the ability of African countries to better know other Africans, to love them, and to respect them. A friend of mine said that the borders of Africa are some of the most clearly defined in the world. All the same, I wish they weren't among the most closed.

The third affliction that we urgently need to combat is our idea of fatalism, specifically a kind of Leibnizian Fatum Mahometanum that absolves us of responsibility for our actions and misdeeds. You're familiar with the common saying here, *ndogalu yalla la*—it is the will of Allah. Yet divine will has never meant an excuse for inaction among those who understand. If we truly believe that some nations are naturally destined to prosper while others are condemned to fail, then we fully deserve our condition. The idea of being poorly served by destiny would then excuse us from the effort of transformation—unless destiny has nothing to do with it and we are capable of radically reshaping our own existence. After all, this same destiny has spared us from typhoons, frequent earthquakes, harsh winters, raging volcanoes, and the ten plagues of Egypt.

We are often told that Africa needs to train scientists, intellectuals, engineers, and healthcare workers in a strictly utilitarian sense. I agree with this. But what good are they to us if they are incapable of thinking for themselves? There is no worse fatalism than that of the expert. The solution to major pandemics will not come from Western laboratories. It's up to our own experts to find ways to harness Africa's vast botanical arsenal. For decades now, we have transformed our resources using only methods taught to us by outsiders. African genius exists, but it's up to us to awaken it. When we take matters into our own hands, we will no longer hear statements about a head of state spoken of in terms such as, "if he is there, it is the will of God or the ancestors."

The last point I would like to mention is the cult of the leader. By personalizing leadership to an extreme degree, we have blown the idea of respect completely out of proportion. Anyone obsessed with his own greatness should make that greatness undeniable. With that in mind, can you look us in the eye and say that you are the greatest? Is the charge of insulting the head of state that you brandish before us daily really an offense, when we are regular witnesses to your pettiness and the erratic behavior of your court? Yes, Mr. President, we have lost respect because you have lost sight of your role. Not long ago, you were the living embodiment of the man we had all been waiting for. You had an admirable combination of patriotism and competence, and you seemed like the type of leader whose courage, tenacity, intelligence, and wide expertise could inspire an entire generation to work hard. Furthermore, your unwavering dignity seemed like a guiding principle for our country. When we entered the new millennium as a full-fledged nation, your success—about which there was no doubt—was to serve as concrete proof that yes, it was possible; an African country could follow the same trajectory as the Four Asian Tigers, the emerging nations of the former communist bloc, or the rentier states of the oil economy. At least, that's what you led us to believe.

I would like to share a personal anecdote. As a child, I once overheard a conversation between my parents. They were talking about entrusting someone with the fate of an entire country. I didn't understand what that meant, but I remember thinking that if my mother was standing up to my father, which she almost never did, then the stakes must be incredibly high. I only heard them disagree like this twice in my childhood. The first time was when my father said he was going to quit his public service job to try his luck abroad. The second time was on that memorable afternoon. My mother is a down-to-earth woman; she has the pragmatism of someone who grew up with the urgency of daily survival. She is the opposite of my idealistic father, who developed a belief in the honor and nobility of great men. I didn't fully understand it at the time, but I remember that after my father left, my mother told me that the people would have to choose a government. She said that the man she called "The Professor" should be president instead of the one who was currently in office. The president? Yes. The Professor had promised that if he became president, he would make rice and meat affordable for all families. We weren't hungry ourselves, but my mother explained that it wasn't just about us—that it was about the people. It was the leader's job to take care of the people, which was exactly what The Professor said he would do. That's why she wanted The Professor to win. I will always remember my mother listening to the election results on the radio while the rest of the family was still asleep. I remember the cold anger and disappointment when we found out the president had won again the next day. There was talk of stolen results, of voting instructions given to certain communities. She also said something that would haunt me for a long time: "This country will never be in the hands of someone who deserves it." Maybe she said it in the heat of anger, but I understood from her words that political victory is never synonymous with moral worth.

Thanks to my mother, I grew up with a certain affection for rebels, for those who oppose the established order. The chivalrous image of The Professor resonated deeply with me, the eternal underdog, the passionate champion of the weak, the symbol of the people. I was thrilled when

I witnessed the tremendous momentum that carried The Professor to the top many years later. All the hope he had crystallized over decades finally took shape. A few years later, my mother's misplaced faith taught me the dangers of placing the hopes of a nation in the hands of a single man.

I don't know the true extent of my mother's disappointment when The Professor turned out to be one of the worst presidents in our history. To be honest, the only thing that matters is the lesson my adolescent conscience finally learned: Caesar's promises are only binding for those who believe in them. Still, I wanted you to know that my mother has since given up voting altogether. That's the second lesson to be learned from this story. While political alternation has been hailed as the best guarantee of a healthy democratic spirit in our country, this Professor-President—the very symbol of that alternation—managed to discredit the office and convince my mother that politics is synonymous with corruption.

Later, I asked my father why he had supported the sitting president when everyone at home saw The Professor as a hero. He did not have anything against The Professor, but he did say this: "To lead a nation, a man must be capable of lucidity."

In a way, both my parents were right in their perceptions. Ultimately, their desires and expectations were the same. Unfortunately, we are still on a quest for a leader who can meet those expectations. In any case, what I had already felt as a child, but was still unable to articulate clearly, came up more than once in my conversations with my father. He always told me that we were no better than any other African country, and that our only saving grace is that our leaders, despite their shortcomings, have managed to retain some of the lucidity needed to run a country. He also added that the day these leaders lose their lucidity, we will sink to the level of the worst dictatorships in the world. My father is a wise man. I have always wondered why lucidity appeared in his discourse, as the primary quality of a statesman. As I grew up, I realized that most of the qualities required for good leadership have to do with lucidity: intelligence, consensus, courage, truth, vision, generosity, foresight. Pair any word denoting the capacity to govern with lucidity, and you will see that it is either an avatar of it or a necessary complement.

I realized, while watching you evolve in your role over the years, that despite my respect for the institution you represent, you have never prioritized lucidity. I am reminded of the words of René Char: "Lucidity is the wound closest to the sun." In the exercise of power there is a gravity that is akin to suffering. And yet it seems like you think *ruling* rhymes with *pleasure*. Of course, I could be wrong, but there are some things I will never understand about your conception of power. But make no mistake: political judgment is never final. You will appear again before the tribunal of history. Nothing can spare you from the reality of your record, not the image you project or the "clean slate" you try to attain in international organizations after leaving office. You have failed due to your inability to uphold the principles that brought you to power. With all the controversy surrounding your actions as President, we cannot pretend that you were the statesman we were hoping for. I would even go so far as to say that never in the history of our country has a president been so out of touch with the concerns of ordinary people. Maybe I'm wrong, Mr. President. But you certainly gave the impression that you're only interested in satisfying your enormous appetite for money and power. Your friends, your family, and your name are so closely tied to the management of our country that all we see is a man with his crew of zealots and sycophants who, in their devotion to the prince's will, are completely cut off from the people. You have convinced me—the artist, the poet, the useless voice—that I will not, in my lifetime, see the Africa I dream of. What's the point of dreaming if the role of African head of state is such a parody?

Mr. President, today I understand my mother's disappointment. I'm even beginning to wonder if she and I are cut from the same cloth. Am I naïve or unreasonable to believe that it is not so difficult to be honest, patriotic, and competent when one wants to become president? I see the noble qualities I've just listed in your political opponents. And do you know what worries me most, Mr. President? It is that these qualities, however firmly ingrained in your opponents, risk being consumed by the exercise of power when their turn comes. The most admirable of opponents remains so only for the duration of opposition. This is because you, like The Professor before you, are proof that deception is the common language of the men and women who seek to sedate the masses. ▪

LETTER FIVE

Mr. President,

I received the message delivered by your emissary, the mayor of our town, the very man you parachuted into our community against our will not so long ago. I never seriously imagined that, from your lofty perch, you would be able to hear even a faint echo of my cry, much less respond. I hoped for it, but I didn't believe it would happen. And yet, you heard me. "I understood your message perfectly: you would like my pen to be used in the service of law and order." Those were the words. Were you aware that this same slogan has been used as a pretext by the worst governments in the world?

My writings, it seems, have the effect of corrupting the youth and threatening national security. My writings! You see, I never thought that writing could play a decisive role in the struggle for truth. I was under the impression that in Africa—where free speech is confiscated by self-styled prophets and charlatans—it would be futile to try to complain or express oneself in writing. Even more so as a means to be heard. And yet, you heard me. I am not worried about thinly veiled threats. I am not afraid. Everyone who has chosen to speak out publicly is familiar with the indecent bargain they have to make: serve, remain silent, or pay the price of dissent. I am ready. You have revived ancient methods to ensure that all public discourse about you becomes praise. Those who refuse to play the game know the price. Our prisons have never been so full—of opponents, of demonstrators, of people who disobey. They do not disobey you, or even the law. They disobey senselessness. They defy outdated laws that no longer reflect the spirit of law—orders whose legal and ethical foundations are impossible to decode. Your perception of criminal law would be laughable if freedom and human dignity didn't depend on it. We could have seen it as just another example of a grotesque judicial farce. But these are our lives, and that compels us to be outraged. Our national narrative, rooted in the pursuit of justice, freedom, and human dignity, is being torn apart in your hands. Despite being legitimate expressions of dissent, peaceful protests are systematically met with brutal repression. Images of security forces abusing their power against children armed only with courage and romantic patriotism, tear away the illusion of peace that envelops our nation. You have transformed the law of the people into the law of the jungle. You have transformed fragile judicial institutions into your own personal vise. No more opposition, no more freedom of speech, no more justice. Now, it's time to take responsibility and understand the true meaning of revolt. It is the assertion of a moral code that stands above written law, whether you approve or not. When tyranny threatens the nation, the citizen is entitled to say, "Enough."

Only one thing is superior to the law: justice. Can we speak of justice, Mr. President, when those who disagree no longer have the right to express their opinions? Can we speak of justice when newspapers, radio stations, TV channels, and websites are all silenced? When the voice of the people, which should resound in the streets and the media, is smothered by a hand that is no longer disguised? Can we speak of justice when journalists, artists, and activists are imprisoned for an article, a concert, or a flyer? Can we speak of justice when the entire penal system is manipulated—without nuance—to monitor, control, repress, and erase any expression of dissatisfaction? Can we speak of justice when detainees are denied the right to defense and held indefinitely for investigations that never occur? Can we speak of justice when citizens are murdered in cold blood, and their killers, because they are somewhat close to you, are never held accountable? Lawyers and judges are becoming fed up with rigged trials, careless processes, deliberate procedural flaws, fabricated evidence (often incriminating), bribed witnesses, manufactured offenses, and dictated convictions. These do not point to a malfunctioning justice system or the manipulation of its actors. No. These are simply the defining characteristics of a dictatorship.

The word has been spoken, Mr. President. We are not—and must not be—a dictatorship. But sometimes a country founded on the rule of law deviates from it to such an extent that it can no longer reasonably be seen as such. We must then brand it with the mark of monstrosity. We are not a dictatorship, but we have become a reflection of one in the mirror. And today, you are the face of that reflection.

A state may cloak itself in elections, democratic tradition, diplomatic triumphs, and respectable spokespeople. But its true nature is always revealed by the people who wake up every morning under the weight of its misdeeds. We are now developing the same reflexes and behaviors as those who live in the most authoritarian regimes in the world. It has become dangerous to speak out. And when speech is threatened, freedom is already dead. We have reached the point where those who go out to a peaceful protest cannot be certain of returning home alive. For the first time, words like "public safety" and "state security" have become leitmotifs in official statements. Why?

You are the first President to trample on an inalienable principle in any self-respecting democracy: the right to information. The fact that our country has been facing a complete shutdown of communication networks for weeks, that certain cities have been deliberately cut off from the rest of the country, that citizens are prevented from leaving their homes because they might take to the streets—this means that this country is under lockdown. This is the new norm our leaders have established: to suppress freedom and restrict free speech.

Until people find in the deepest reserves of their soul the courage to revolt and put an end to this monster, it can appear almost normal. This is because a dictatorship is known for its ability to normalize the monstrosity of the state, using a seemingly normal control structure with a normal police force, a normal justice system, and a normal administration. Those who serve your system are normal people, normal police officers and judges, normal teachers, and normal religious figures. After all, let's not forget that normalcy is the foundation of accepting an everyday reality that is anything but. We are not used to being silent. We are not used to hiding. We are not used to distrusting our neighbor. Yet these attitudes have become normal. Conversely, opposing the system has become an abnormal, even marginal act. To oppose it, you must accept the label of conspirator, in league with obscure foreign forces.

You must be a terrorist, a separatist, an anti-republican, a troublemaker, an unemployed person, a drug addict, or a madman. You must be abnormal to say that another system is possible.

Yet, within this banality of evil, the resistance has patiently organized itself to the point that it is now you who seems to be afraid. The number of arbitrary arrests has increased, political deaths are counted in the dozens, and the borders have become more impenetrable than ever. Despite the increasingly aggressive response to our cries, we are still here, standing tall, and growing in numbers. At sporting events, in religious ceremonies, in other countries—wherever citizens have a chance to gather—they seize the opportunity to loudly proclaim their opposition to what you represent. You have canceled your trips. You remain locked in your palace. God alone knows what your heart is telling you as this muffled wave looms outside your gates. ▪

POSTSCRIPTUM

Mr. President,

I write to you one last time to thank you, despite everything, for having allowed me to express through you what all of Africa's youth long to say to their leaders. I am grateful that you have heard these words. Perhaps this is what has fundamentally changed today in the political landscape on our continent. It has become impossible to stifle speech, despite your desperate attempts. And now that everything has been brought to light, you can no longer pretend not to know what your presence means for your fellow citizens. The noise is deafening. The light is harsh. You stand exposed in it. You are accountable now—either you accept it or you flee from it, but you cannot claim ignorance.

Over the past few months, we've heard all sorts of conflicting information about your intentions to step down. Some believe you wish to enter history as one of the rare African presidents to relinquish power voluntarily and leave of your own accord. Others believe, on the contrary, that you wish to be re-elected. For the umpteenth time. It would seem that you could achieve that by simply making the country ungovernable for others. Your silence, which we've all grown accustomed to, has left the door wide open to speculation. We are therefore not immune to a protracted constitutional crisis that could lead to social unrest, to the usual imprisonments, to the same demonstrations and the same repression, to the same pre-election chaos, to a state of emergency that would justify your staying in office, to the withdrawal of your main opponents, and pave your way forward. It's enough to make your head spin, but in Africa, we know this story by heart.

While listening to the radio this morning, I gleaned that the people of the soil still hold you in very high esteem. Opposition to your rule is limited to social media and a few major cities. A negligible quantity, it would seem. One of your ministers even claimed (without batting an eye) that 80% of the votes would be yours if you decided to run. That's not just an election victory; that's a kiss on the lips from our fellow citizens. Shame on the dissidents hiding in the "20%" of recalcitrants!

However, in my humble opinion, you would be better advised to leave. We have reached the end of the road, Mr. President. Contrary to appearances, polls, and partisan posturing, your downfall is predictable, and I will tell you why. You have been here too long; you have pushed things as far as history will allow. This is not a matter of politics, as some have claimed, or a matter of interpreting sovereign powers. It is not even about the legitimacy of the legal patchwork your parliamentary majority is so skilled at. It's much simpler than that. It's a matter of humanity. And that is why I refuse to believe the rumors that you intend to remain in power until the end of your life. We never signed that contract, and no republic is meant to accompany its President to the grave. I am convinced you have enough lucidity to understand that you cannot continue to ignore the call of history. I hope you will have some respect for the good fortune that brought you to power in the first place by stepping down. The joys of ruling will never justify the price of bloodshed. Because blood would flow in torrents if your plan came to fruition. And no poll would change that.

Your inner circle is lying to you. They won't tell you about the adolescents determined to defy your security and defense forces. They will never tell you about the widow ready to throw herself against the gates of your palace in the spirit of sacrifice. They won't tell you that, across the country, resistance cells are taking shape, strikes are being planned, and underground publications pass from hand to hand to challenge your legitimacy and say that the nation has had enough. Mr. President, your faithful will never tell you this, because now, even your own shoes are afraid of you. This is the sign of a man backed into a corner. You see enemies and conspiracies everywhere you turn. The voice of reason hidden deep within your conscience (if you have one) will command you to step down, because the writing is on the wall. This time, not even your luck will endorse yet another term. Knowing when to leave isn't the same thing as giving up—it means recognizing hard limits and understanding when exceeding them would be an unnecessary risk. A risk to one's legacy, one's reputation, and above all, one's life.

And life, dear President, has so much to offer, even when a seemingly endless political chapter comes to a close. Provided one leaves when the time has come. One always wonders why this historical evidence is harder to accept in Africa than elsewhere. Let us take inspiration from those who stand as exceptions: Léopold Sédar Senghor, Julius Nyerere, Amadou Toumani Touré, Liamine Zeroual . . . They were not perfect, but one day, they had the clarity to accept the idea of an end. That is what made them great in my eyes. We must also remember those who did not know how to leave. Prison, exile, death—worse still, humiliation, hatred, and damnation.

Some installed a son, brother, or cousin in their place. Others appointed a comrade-in-arms, or a compliant prime minister, or simply died a peaceful death. But what did the people gain?

Look at these viziers, these incompetent dauphins, who, for having enjoyed the favor of the Sun King, find themselves propelled to the summit, in defiance of logic and common sense. The world we live in has made the unspeakable acceptable. Unloved but feared daddy's boys, dandies on perpetual vacation, and upstart princes who have never once earned a privilege can end up with the destiny of an entire nation in their hands overnight. We see them go from private yachts to the People's House, from the VIP lounge to the National Assembly, from charity galas to election campaigns, from ski slopes to cabinet meetings. We've swallowed so many of these political serpents, powerless as we were before you. But now we know it's possible to refuse.

We are the Africa in which power has been passed down from father to son (never from mother to daughter, have you noticed?). A continent where absolute idiots presided over the fates of millions, as if ruling were nothing more than an internship. We are that world in which onomastic continuity was not an unattainable dream, but an implicit law inscribed in the family constitution. We are the place where elections were rigged so that scatterbrained successors could perpetuate the grand works of a dead man. We are the people who have slept peacefully through these practices until this morning.

We've decided that we will no longer accept this. We've shown you in countless ways that we no longer want any part of that world. Whether you are wise enough to understand this new reality remains to be seen. Mr. President, I implore you: respect the true will of your people. Do not listen to those who tell you to hold on. You no longer should. You no longer can. I say this not only because of your tenuous hold on power, but also because your fellow citizens no longer want you. Hear them, if you cannot see them. Fear them, if you cannot love them. Africans are now ready to fight, and this movement is not going to stop anytime soon. It is a current, a wave, a tsunami that will sweep you away whether you like it or not.

I saw you on TV the other day talking about youth violence, about these mobs of delinquents who threaten the safety of people and property. I even heard you talk about the loss of values like respect. I cannot disagree with you: the youth who stand so boldly before you today are not the same ones you once knew. So, what happened? Why have these young people become so insolent, so aggressive, so violent? Consider Plato's words:

> "*When the young men despise the laws because they no longer recognize any authority above them, then at last, in all its beauty and excess, tyranny is born.*"*

To many in your generation, African youth seem to lack direction. We often hear that respect for elders no

* Translator's Note: Line from Plato's *Republic*, transl. by Benjamin Jowett

longer means anything. In the past, a son who disagreed would simply remain silent. In that respect, you are right. You are also right that African values are not the same as those of other countries whose leaders are reviled and dragged through the mud, without any regard for their age or position. You are astonished that, like Western youth, we are impatient young bucks, demanding for our countries the same privileges as the rest of the world. We seem completely disconnected from African history, and this bothers you. While there is some truth to this idea, there is a fundamental element whose deeper meaning you can hardly begin to grasp.

Mr. President, most of us were born after 1960. This might not mean much to you, for many whisper that you have little affinity with history. It is simply to say that we belong to a generation that did not experience colonization. As such, we have learned to look at the world, if not as free men and women, then at least with a visceral hatred of servitude. Today, when I encounter the world and look it in the eye, I feel no desire to lower my head and let it continue to trample me, as was the case with my ancestors. Quite the opposite. But the world still looks at me as if I were a colonized subject. It has gathered humanity under the flag of globalization, but continues to consider me a pariah, an untouchable. In its eyes, I am the dregs of humanity and the one in whom all the peoples of the earth see their slave. The world speaks to me as if, from our shared history, only the lingering traces of an alienation once suffered and now accepted could remain. I have often been astonished that this world, which I otherwise cherish, has not yet realized that I have become its equal again, that the chapters of slavery and colonization (which all people have experienced to some degree, but to which we are bound as if we had a monopoly on them) have closed, and that I now refuse to bear on my forehead the mark of eternal damnation. This genomic branding, that makes me the burden of humanity in its quest for the future, fills me with extreme indignation.

I want to show the world who we are. The world that persists in weighing us down with its ancient contempt and condescension . . . Yes, Mr. President, we want to fight back. As I watch you, however, I realize that it will be difficult for us to shake off the suffocating role of the black sheep that has been forced upon us. It will be difficult, and I accuse you, Mr. President, you and your ilk, of being the ones who forcibly keep us in this straitjacket of systematic humiliation, endemic poverty, degrading disease, indignity, and a total loss of self-esteem. It is you who preside over our destinies and to whom fate has given the formidable and exhilarating mission of speaking on our behalf. You have no regard whatsoever for the respect that we Africans demand from the world. You are still haunted by the defeats our ancestors suffered; you think, you speak, you act, you see the world as defeated men. How then can we rise to the challenge and force the hand of a world that is still reluctant to offer us a place at the table?

It is very hard for me to accept that my country is being relegated to the cargo holds of the human galley, when for so long I have claimed my place on the deck of historical progress. As I study the world from every angle, I see no youth more intelligent, more cultured, more inspired, or more creative than that of my country. We are the equals of the other children of the world—in intention, in spirit, in creative ability. Why don't we have their respect? Why don't we have their consideration? Why do we so rarely have the opportunity to show we are their equals?

African youth hesitate to embrace their brilliance because they lack immediate points of reference to counter the denigration of their genius. At the crossroads of the Whole-World, it is the African youth who are subjected to the painful ordeal of obtaining a visa; and when they finally obtain that pass key, they must endure the degradation of searches that treat every orifice of their bodies as the hiding place of some nameless horror threatening the rest of humanity. African youth have become a color, a smell, a virus, a disease, a danger—even to those who invite them in and claim friendship. How did they come to be seen as potential bombs or poisons? Why are they kept at the margins of civilization before they've even had a chance to prove themselves? The presence of our youth in major scientific, artistic, and sporting events is not a given. Their participation raises questions about why they are there and through which charitable program. They are the ones who are believed to be incapable of understanding the world as an abstraction, and who can only travel the world to work their asses off in the most degrading jobs, to escape the chronic poverty that curses their homeland. For our youth, no fault, weakness, or oversight is ever forgiven. The most mediocre individuals elsewhere dare to compare themselves to our youth, confusing the nation with the individual. A Togolese doctor may equal a French nurse. A Senegalese law professor is another country's notary clerk. We have been hardened by an obligation to do more to meet the same standards. In the eyes of others, we have never been the kind of travelers who should be generously welcomed and encouraged to return. We are the embodiment of the immigrant worker who must be kicked, bludgeoned with the butt of a rifle, hurled from bridges, humiliated, and murdered in the rear of an airliner to ensure he never comes back to claim the bread stolen by yesterday's invaders. We will continue to roll the Sisyphean stone of our human dignity uphill, like our brothers and sisters of the Whole-World, whom people imagine to be crude, savage, naïve, overly emotional, naked, and still entangled in the reticulated branches of the maternal coconut tree.

And so, Mr. President, to preserve the strength to keep fighting and to continue believing in our perpetually mortgaged future, I turn to you, urging you to assume your historical responsibility in dismantling this image of Africa. This work began several decades ago. Political resolve was essential to its development, but ultimately, you have been its main saboteur. We are ready to try again. I have concluded that if my country—like the other African nations—carries so little weight on the international stage, even though its people excel whenever they are offered opportunities, it is because it is sick with its political elites. And who better embodies this elite: devoid of genius, lacking moral character, incapable of setting us on the path to progress and dignity? Of course, people will bring up a plethora of circumstantial, geopolitical, or even natural factors. So be it. But it seems to me that every nation that has become an example of collective success (including African nations before the era of decline), did so by relying on the political genius, visionary force, nation-building talent, and innovative capacity of their leaders. I believe that every people harbors within itself and its collective imagination all the resources needed for technological, economic, artistic, and moral progress—not to resemble others, but to achieve just as much.

I understand now that you are the problem. If African countries have been floundering in disgrace since I was born, it has less to do with their shared heritage than the fools who lead them. We, the young people of Africa, are not asking for the moon. We are not asking you to erase, with a wave of a magic wand, all the backwardness accumulated from centuries of systematic plunder, complete denial, deliberate obstruction, continuous sabotage, lies, massacres, deportations, complexes, and perpetuated divisions. No, we are not asking you alone, here and now, to repair the damage wrought by a meticulously planned enterprise of destruction set in motion before your forefathers were born, and which the West, beneath its humanist mask, continues to prolong. What we ask of you and your peers is to try—and to try in earnest. Try to restore true dignity to the continent. Try to become leaders capable of instilling new energy in your people. Try to be political figures with enough strength and confidence to defend African interests and negotiate with your counterparts as equals. Try to find reliable solutions to fight diseases, make education accessible, lift people out of their difficulties, and put an end to wars and corruption. We will help you. But please, do something, or else give us back our country.

I am therefore writing to you today to express my concern one last time. I feel that there is a clear disconnect, Mr. President, between you, our leaders, and the African youth. Your record alone suffices to prove everything I have just written. That record, which I am about to lay out now, is dismal, and you will be held accountable for it for all eternity. Believe me, if I could find reasons to praise you, I would have done so. But you have failed, like so many of your peers. There will always be, in a burst of distinctly African charity, reasons to absolve you of your incompetence in lifting up your country. That is how we treat our tormentors.

I would like to end this final letter by telling you how bitterly disappointed I am that the lust for power has become the driving force of political life. The people put so much hope in you. You were not expected to bring happiness to everyone, but at least to ensure that no one was overwhelmed by despair. Instead, you have deepened that despair. While our nation loses billions, the embezzlers continue to dance around the corpse. Like you, none of them will be held accountable; like you, none of them will ever be satisfied. So it goes in Africa.

But, sir, the time has come for you to understand that we will stand in your way, for we have resolved, from this day forward, to hold you accountable. In the name of these new prerogatives, we have declared you no longer fit to stand. Being President is a moment, not a lifetime. The door to another destiny is standing open before you. It is for you to choose whether it leads to retirement or to ruin. And Mr. President, don't bother trying to close the door behind you. History will take care of that. ▪

www.ingramcontent.com/pod-product-compliance
Ingram Content Group UK Ltd.
Pitfield, Milton Keynes, MK11 3LW, UK
UKHW042013190726
13854UKWH00005B/2267

9 798994 894118